50 Premium Milk Meals for Dinner

By: Kelly Johnson

Table of Contents

- Creamy Chicken Alfredo
- Mushroom Risotto with Milk
- Milk-Braised Pork Belly
- Classic Mac and Cheese with Creamy Milk Sauce
- Creamy Garlic Parmesan Chicken
- Milk-Based Tomato Basil Soup
- Creamy Spinach and Ricotta Stuffed Chicken
- Beef Stroganoff with Milk
- Creamy Shrimp Scampi
- Milk-Poached Salmon
- Creamy Broccoli and Cheddar Casserole
- Chicken and Mushroom Milk Pie
- Milk-Infused Baked Ziti
- Creamy Tuscan Chicken
- Grilled Cheese Sandwich with Milk-Based Tomato Soup
- Milk-Poached Cod with Herbs
- Chicken and Milk-Creamed Spinach
- Smoked Salmon Milk Soup
- Beef and Milk Stew
- Creamy Fettuccine Alfredo
- Milk and Herb Marinated Chicken Thighs
- Creamy Cauliflower Soup with Milk
- Milk-Infused Potato Gratin
- Coconut Milk Chicken Curry
- Macadamia-Crusted Chicken with Milk Sauce
- Creamy Sun-Dried Tomato Pasta
- Milk-Cooked Risotto with Shrimp
- Dairy-Free Milk Shepherd's Pie
- Braised Short Ribs with Milk and Herbs
- Milk and Honey Glazed Chicken
- Creamy Leek and Potato Soup
- Roasted Chicken with Milk Sauce
- Milk-Cooked Pork Tenderloin
- Parmesan Chicken with Milk Cream Sauce
- Creamy Vegetable Pasta Bake

- Honey-Glazed Salmon with Milk Drizzle
- Milk and Dijon Chicken
- Spaghetti Carbonara with Milk
- Smoked Gouda and Milk Mac and Cheese
- Chicken Marsala with Milk Cream Sauce
- Milk-Cooked Risotto Primavera
- Garlic and Herb Milk-Cooked Lamb
- Creamy Chive Mashed Potatoes with Milk
- Milk-Braised Veal with Vegetables
- Grilled Chicken with Creamy Milk Sauce
- Milk-Poached Lobster Tails
- Creamy Risotto with Peas and Milk
- Braised Lamb Shanks in Milk
- Milk and Tomato Braised Chicken
- Creamy Parmesan Garlic Chicken and Rice

Creamy Chicken Alfredo

Ingredients:

- 1 lb chicken breast, sliced into strips
- 2 tbsp butter
- 2 cups heavy cream
- 1 cup whole milk
- 2 cups grated Parmesan cheese
- 2 garlic cloves, minced
- 8 oz fettuccine pasta
- Salt and pepper to taste
- Fresh parsley, chopped (optional)

Instructions:

1. Cook fettuccine pasta according to package directions. Drain and set aside.
2. In a large skillet, melt butter over medium heat. Add chicken strips and cook until browned and cooked through, about 7-8 minutes. Remove from the skillet and set aside.
3. In the same skillet, add minced garlic and cook for 1 minute until fragrant.
4. Pour in the heavy cream and milk, bringing it to a simmer. Stir constantly.
5. Once the sauce thickens slightly, add Parmesan cheese, salt, and pepper. Stir until the cheese melts and the sauce becomes smooth.
6. Add the cooked pasta and chicken into the skillet, tossing to coat everything in the creamy sauce.
7. Garnish with chopped parsley before serving.

Mushroom Risotto with Milk

Ingredients:

- 1 cup Arborio rice
- 2 tbsp butter
- 1 onion, finely chopped
- 2 garlic cloves, minced
- 2 cups mushrooms, sliced
- 4 cups chicken or vegetable broth
- 1 cup whole milk
- 1/2 cup grated Parmesan cheese
- Salt and pepper to taste
- Fresh parsley, chopped (optional)

Instructions:

1. In a large pan, melt butter over medium heat. Add onion and garlic and sauté for 2-3 minutes until softened.
2. Add sliced mushrooms and cook until tender, about 5 minutes.
3. Stir in Arborio rice and cook for 1-2 minutes to lightly toast it.
4. Gradually add broth, one cup at a time, stirring constantly and allowing each addition to be absorbed before adding more.
5. After the broth is fully absorbed, add the milk and continue stirring until the rice is creamy and tender.
6. Stir in Parmesan cheese, salt, and pepper. Garnish with fresh parsley before serving.

Milk-Braised Pork Belly

Ingredients:

- 1 lb pork belly, cut into chunks
- 2 tbsp vegetable oil
- 1 onion, chopped
- 2 garlic cloves, minced
- 1 cup whole milk
- 1/2 cup chicken broth
- 1 tbsp soy sauce
- 1 tbsp brown sugar
- Salt and pepper to taste

Instructions:

1. In a large pot, heat vegetable oil over medium heat. Brown pork belly chunks on all sides, about 5-7 minutes. Remove and set aside.
2. In the same pot, add onion and garlic and cook until softened, about 3 minutes.
3. Add milk, chicken broth, soy sauce, and brown sugar. Stir to combine.
4. Return the pork belly to the pot, season with salt and pepper, and bring to a simmer.
5. Cover the pot, reduce the heat, and let simmer for 1-1.5 hours until the pork is tender and the sauce thickens.
6. Serve the pork belly with mashed potatoes or rice, spooning the sauce over the top.

Classic Mac and Cheese with Creamy Milk Sauce

Ingredients:

- 8 oz elbow macaroni
- 2 cups whole milk
- 1 1/2 cups shredded cheddar cheese
- 1/2 cup grated Parmesan cheese
- 2 tbsp butter
- 1 tbsp all-purpose flour
- 1/2 tsp mustard powder (optional)
- Salt and pepper to taste

Instructions:

1. Cook macaroni according to package directions. Drain and set aside.
2. In a saucepan, melt butter over medium heat. Add flour and cook for 1-2 minutes to create a roux.
3. Slowly pour in the milk while whisking to avoid lumps. Bring to a simmer and cook for 3-5 minutes until the sauce thickens.
4. Stir in cheddar cheese, Parmesan cheese, mustard powder, salt, and pepper. Continue stirring until the cheese melts and the sauce becomes smooth.
5. Add the cooked macaroni to the sauce and stir to coat evenly.
6. Serve immediately, garnished with additional cheese if desired.

Creamy Garlic Parmesan Chicken

Ingredients:

- 4 boneless, skinless chicken breasts
- 2 tbsp butter
- 4 garlic cloves, minced
- 1 cup heavy cream
- 1/2 cup whole milk
- 1/2 cup grated Parmesan cheese
- Salt and pepper to taste
- Fresh parsley, chopped (optional)

Instructions:

1. In a large skillet, melt butter over medium heat. Season the chicken breasts with salt and pepper, then cook them in the skillet until golden and cooked through, about 7-8 minutes per side. Remove and set aside.
2. In the same skillet, add minced garlic and cook for 1 minute until fragrant.
3. Pour in the heavy cream and milk, scraping any brown bits from the bottom of the skillet.
4. Stir in Parmesan cheese and cook for another 3-5 minutes until the sauce thickens.
5. Return the chicken to the skillet and coat with the creamy sauce.
6. Garnish with fresh parsley and serve over pasta or rice.

Milk-Based Tomato Basil Soup

Ingredients:

- 1 tbsp olive oil
- 1 onion, chopped
- 2 garlic cloves, minced
- 2 cans (14 oz each) diced tomatoes
- 2 cups whole milk
- 1/2 cup vegetable broth
- 1 tbsp dried basil
- Salt and pepper to taste
- Fresh basil leaves for garnish (optional)

Instructions:

1. Heat olive oil in a large pot over medium heat. Add onion and garlic and sauté until softened, about 5 minutes.
2. Add diced tomatoes, milk, vegetable broth, basil, salt, and pepper. Bring the mixture to a simmer.
3. Let simmer for 15-20 minutes, allowing the flavors to combine and the soup to thicken.
4. Use an immersion blender to blend the soup until smooth, or carefully transfer it to a blender.
5. Serve with fresh basil leaves and crusty bread.

Creamy Spinach and Ricotta Stuffed Chicken

Ingredients:

- 4 boneless, skinless chicken breasts
- 1 cup ricotta cheese
- 1/2 cup frozen spinach, thawed and drained
- 1/4 cup grated Parmesan cheese
- 1/2 cup whole milk
- 1 tbsp olive oil
- 1 garlic clove, minced
- Salt and pepper to taste

Instructions:

1. Preheat the oven to 375°F (190°C).
2. In a bowl, combine ricotta cheese, spinach, Parmesan cheese, garlic, salt, and pepper.
3. Slice a pocket into each chicken breast and stuff with the spinach and ricotta mixture.
4. Heat olive oil in a skillet over medium heat. Sear the chicken breasts on both sides until golden, about 4-5 minutes per side.
5. Transfer the chicken to the oven and bake for 20-25 minutes, until the chicken is cooked through.
6. Meanwhile, in the same skillet, add milk and simmer for 5 minutes to create a creamy sauce.
7. Pour the sauce over the stuffed chicken breasts before serving.

Beef Stroganoff with Milk

Ingredients:

- 1 lb beef sirloin, thinly sliced
- 2 tbsp butter
- 1 onion, chopped
- 2 garlic cloves, minced
- 1 cup whole milk
- 1/2 cup beef broth
- 1 tbsp Dijon mustard
- 1/2 tsp paprika
- 1/2 cup sour cream
- Salt and pepper to taste
- Cooked egg noodles for serving

Instructions:

1. Heat butter in a large skillet over medium heat. Add beef and cook until browned, about 5-7 minutes. Remove and set aside.
2. In the same skillet, sauté onion and garlic until softened, about 3 minutes.
3. Stir in beef broth, milk, mustard, paprika, salt, and pepper. Bring to a simmer.
4. Add the beef back to the skillet and simmer for 10-15 minutes, until the sauce thickens.
5. Stir in sour cream and cook for an additional 2-3 minutes.
6. Serve the stroganoff over egg noodles.

Creamy Shrimp Scampi

Ingredients:

- 1 lb shrimp, peeled and deveined
- 2 tbsp butter
- 4 garlic cloves, minced
- 1/2 cup white wine
- 1 cup heavy cream
- 1/4 cup Parmesan cheese
- 1 tbsp lemon juice
- Salt and pepper to taste
- Fresh parsley for garnish
- Cooked pasta for serving

Instructions:

1. In a large skillet, melt butter over medium heat. Add garlic and cook for 1 minute until fragrant.
2. Add shrimp and cook until pink, about 3-4 minutes. Remove the shrimp from the skillet and set aside.
3. Pour in white wine and let it simmer for 2-3 minutes to reduce slightly.
4. Stir in heavy cream and Parmesan cheese, simmering until the sauce thickens.
5. Add the shrimp back to the skillet, along with lemon juice, salt, and pepper.
6. Serve the shrimp scampi over pasta and garnish with fresh parsley.

Milk-Poached Salmon

Ingredients:

- 4 salmon fillets
- 2 cups whole milk
- 1/2 cup water
- 1 tablespoon butter
- 2 garlic cloves, minced
- 1 sprig fresh thyme
- Salt and pepper to taste
- Lemon wedges (for serving)

Instructions:

1. In a wide, shallow pan, combine milk, water, butter, garlic, thyme, salt, and pepper. Bring to a simmer over medium heat.
2. Add the salmon fillets, skin-side down. Reduce the heat to low and poach the salmon for 10-12 minutes, or until it flakes easily with a fork.
3. Remove the salmon fillets from the milk and set them aside.
4. Strain the poaching liquid and serve it as a light sauce over the salmon, garnishing with fresh lemon wedges.

Creamy Broccoli and Cheddar Casserole

Ingredients:

- 4 cups broccoli florets
- 1 1/2 cups shredded sharp cheddar cheese
- 1 cup whole milk
- 1/2 cup breadcrumbs
- 2 tablespoons butter
- 2 tablespoons all-purpose flour
- 1/2 teaspoon garlic powder
- Salt and pepper to taste

Instructions:

1. Preheat the oven to 375°F (190°C). Steam the broccoli florets until tender, about 5-7 minutes. Set aside.
2. In a saucepan, melt butter over medium heat. Add flour and cook for 1-2 minutes to make a roux.
3. Gradually whisk in milk, garlic powder, salt, and pepper. Continue whisking until the sauce thickens, about 5 minutes.
4. Stir in the cheddar cheese until melted and smooth.
5. Combine the broccoli and cheese sauce, then transfer to a greased baking dish. Top with breadcrumbs.
6. Bake for 15-20 minutes until the top is golden and bubbly. Serve hot.

Chicken and Mushroom Milk Pie

Ingredients:

- 1 lb chicken breast, cooked and shredded
- 2 cups mushrooms, sliced
- 1 onion, chopped
- 2 cups whole milk
- 1/4 cup flour
- 1/2 cup frozen peas
- 1 sheet puff pastry (or pie crust)
- 2 tbsp butter
- Salt and pepper to taste

Instructions:

1. Preheat the oven to 375°F (190°C). Roll out the puff pastry to fit your pie dish and set it aside.
2. In a skillet, melt butter over medium heat. Add the onions and cook until soft, about 5 minutes.
3. Add the mushrooms and cook until tender, about 4 minutes.
4. Stir in flour and cook for another minute to make a roux. Gradually pour in milk, whisking until the mixture thickens, about 5-7 minutes.
5. Stir in the shredded chicken and peas. Season with salt and pepper.
6. Pour the filling into the prepared pie crust and cover with the top pastry layer. Trim and seal the edges.
7. Cut slits in the top to allow steam to escape, then bake for 25-30 minutes or until the crust is golden.
8. Let the pie cool slightly before serving.

Milk-Infused Baked Ziti

Ingredients:

- 1 lb ziti pasta
- 2 cups whole milk
- 1 1/2 cups marinara sauce
- 1/2 cup ricotta cheese
- 1 1/2 cups shredded mozzarella cheese
- 1/4 cup grated Parmesan cheese
- 2 tbsp olive oil
- 2 garlic cloves, minced
- Salt and pepper to taste

Instructions:

1. Preheat the oven to 375°F (190°C). Cook the ziti pasta according to package directions and drain.
2. In a skillet, heat olive oil over medium heat. Add garlic and cook for 1 minute until fragrant.
3. Stir in marinara sauce and milk. Bring to a simmer and cook for 5 minutes, then remove from heat.
4. In a large bowl, combine cooked ziti, ricotta cheese, mozzarella cheese, and the sauce mixture. Season with salt and pepper.
5. Pour the mixture into a greased baking dish and top with Parmesan cheese.
6. Bake for 20-25 minutes, or until the cheese is bubbly and golden. Serve hot.

Creamy Tuscan Chicken

Ingredients:

- 4 boneless, skinless chicken breasts
- 1 tbsp olive oil
- 2 cups whole milk
- 1/2 cup sun-dried tomatoes, chopped
- 1/2 cup spinach, chopped
- 2 garlic cloves, minced
- 1/2 cup grated Parmesan cheese
- Salt and pepper to taste

Instructions:

1. Heat olive oil in a large skillet over medium heat. Season chicken breasts with salt and pepper, then cook for 6-7 minutes on each side until golden and cooked through. Remove and set aside.
2. In the same skillet, add garlic and cook for 1 minute. Stir in sun-dried tomatoes, spinach, and milk. Bring to a simmer.
3. Stir in Parmesan cheese and cook until the sauce thickens, about 5 minutes.
4. Return the chicken to the skillet, spoon sauce over the top, and cook for an additional 5 minutes to combine the flavors.
5. Serve the creamy Tuscan chicken over pasta or rice.

Grilled Cheese Sandwich with Milk-Based Tomato Soup

Ingredients:

- **For the soup:**
    - 1 can (14 oz) crushed tomatoes
    - 1 cup whole milk
    - 1/2 cup vegetable broth
    - 1 onion, chopped
    - 1 garlic clove, minced
    - 1 tbsp butter
    - 1/2 tsp sugar
    - Salt and pepper to taste
    - Fresh basil leaves (optional)
- **For the grilled cheese:**
    - 8 slices of bread
    - 4 slices of cheddar cheese
    - 2 tbsp butter

Instructions:

1. **For the soup:** In a saucepan, melt butter over medium heat. Add onion and garlic and cook for 5 minutes until softened.
2. Add crushed tomatoes, milk, vegetable broth, sugar, salt, and pepper. Bring to a simmer and cook for 15 minutes.
3. Use an immersion blender to blend the soup until smooth. Adjust seasoning as needed and keep warm.
4. **For the grilled cheese:** Butter one side of each slice of bread. Place cheese between two slices of bread, buttered side out.
5. Grill sandwiches in a skillet over medium heat until golden brown on both sides and the cheese is melted.
6. Serve the grilled cheese with the tomato soup and garnish with fresh basil if desired.

Milk-Poached Cod with Herbs

Ingredients:

- 4 cod fillets
- 2 cups whole milk
- 1/2 cup water
- 2 tbsp butter
- 2 garlic cloves, minced
- 1 sprig fresh rosemary
- 1 sprig fresh thyme
- Salt and pepper to taste
- Lemon wedges (for serving)

Instructions:

1. In a shallow pan, combine milk, water, butter, garlic, rosemary, thyme, salt, and pepper. Bring to a simmer over medium heat.
2. Add the cod fillets and poach for 10-12 minutes, or until the fish flakes easily with a fork.
3. Remove the fish and set aside. Strain the poaching liquid and serve over the cod fillets.
4. Garnish with lemon wedges and serve with steamed vegetables or rice.

Chicken and Milk-Creamed Spinach

Ingredients:

- 4 boneless, skinless chicken breasts
- 2 cups spinach, chopped
- 1 cup whole milk
- 1/2 cup heavy cream
- 2 tbsp butter
- 2 garlic cloves, minced
- 1/4 tsp nutmeg
- Salt and pepper to taste

Instructions:

1. Cook chicken breasts in a skillet over medium heat until golden and cooked through. Remove and set aside.
2. In the same skillet, melt butter and sauté garlic for 1 minute until fragrant.
3. Add spinach and cook until wilted, about 3 minutes. Stir in milk, cream, nutmeg, salt, and pepper.
4. Let the sauce simmer and thicken for 5 minutes.
5. Return the chicken to the skillet and coat with the creamy spinach sauce.
6. Serve the chicken with mashed potatoes or rice.

Smoked Salmon Milk Soup

Ingredients:

- 1 cup smoked salmon, chopped
- 2 cups whole milk
- 1/2 cup vegetable broth
- 1 tbsp butter
- 1 onion, chopped
- 1 garlic clove, minced
- 1/2 cup heavy cream
- 1 tbsp fresh dill, chopped
- Salt and pepper to taste

Instructions:

1. In a pot, melt butter over medium heat. Add onion and garlic and cook until softened, about 5 minutes.
2. Stir in vegetable broth and milk, bringing it to a simmer.
3. Add the smoked salmon and let the soup simmer for 5-7 minutes.
4. Stir in heavy cream and fresh dill. Season with salt and pepper.
5. Serve the soup hot, garnished with additional dill.

Beef and Milk Stew

Ingredients:

- 1 lb beef stew meat, cubed
- 2 cups whole milk
- 1 cup beef broth
- 2 carrots, sliced
- 1 onion, chopped
- 2 garlic cloves, minced
- 1/2 cup frozen peas
- 1 tablespoon flour
- 2 tablespoons butter
- 2 sprigs thyme
- Salt and pepper to taste

Instructions:

1. In a large pot, melt butter over medium heat. Add beef stew meat and cook until browned on all sides. Remove and set aside.
2. In the same pot, add onion, carrots, and garlic, and cook for 5-7 minutes until softened.
3. Sprinkle flour over the vegetables and stir to coat. Cook for 1 minute.
4. Gradually pour in beef broth and milk, stirring to combine. Add thyme, salt, and pepper.
5. Return the beef to the pot, bring the stew to a simmer, and cook for 1-2 hours until the beef is tender.
6. Stir in frozen peas during the last 5 minutes of cooking.
7. Serve hot with crusty bread.

Creamy Fettuccine Alfredo

Ingredients:

- 12 oz fettuccine pasta
- 2 cups whole milk
- 1/2 cup heavy cream
- 1 cup grated Parmesan cheese
- 2 tablespoons butter
- 2 garlic cloves, minced
- Salt and pepper to taste
- Fresh parsley (for garnish)

Instructions:

1. Cook the fettuccine pasta according to package directions, then drain.
2. In a large skillet, melt butter over medium heat. Add garlic and cook for 1 minute.
3. Pour in the milk and heavy cream, stirring to combine. Bring to a simmer and cook for 5 minutes, letting the sauce thicken.
4. Stir in the Parmesan cheese until melted and smooth. Season with salt and pepper.
5. Add the cooked fettuccine to the sauce and toss to coat.
6. Serve hot, garnished with fresh parsley.

Milk and Herb Marinated Chicken Thighs

Ingredients:

- 4 chicken thighs, bone-in, skin-on
- 1 cup whole milk
- 2 tablespoons olive oil
- 1 tablespoon lemon juice
- 2 garlic cloves, minced
- 1 teaspoon fresh rosemary, chopped
- 1 teaspoon fresh thyme, chopped
- Salt and pepper to taste

Instructions:

1. In a bowl, whisk together milk, olive oil, lemon juice, garlic, rosemary, thyme, salt, and pepper.
2. Place chicken thighs in a shallow dish and pour the marinade over the chicken. Cover and refrigerate for at least 2 hours, preferably overnight.
3. Preheat the oven to 375°F (190°C). Remove the chicken from the marinade and discard the marinade.
4. Place the chicken thighs on a baking sheet and bake for 35-40 minutes, or until the skin is crispy and the chicken is cooked through.
5. Serve with roasted vegetables or a salad.

Creamy Cauliflower Soup with Milk

Ingredients:

- 1 medium cauliflower, chopped
- 1 onion, chopped
- 2 cups whole milk
- 1 cup vegetable broth
- 2 tablespoons butter
- 2 garlic cloves, minced
- 1/2 teaspoon nutmeg
- Salt and pepper to taste
- Fresh parsley (for garnish)

Instructions:

1. In a large pot, melt butter over medium heat. Add onion and garlic, and cook for 5 minutes until softened.
2. Add cauliflower, vegetable broth, and enough water to cover the cauliflower. Bring to a boil, then reduce heat and simmer for 15-20 minutes, until the cauliflower is tender.
3. Use an immersion blender or transfer the mixture to a blender to puree the soup until smooth.
4. Return the soup to the pot, stir in milk, nutmeg, salt, and pepper. Simmer for an additional 5 minutes.
5. Serve hot, garnished with fresh parsley.

Milk-Infused Potato Gratin

Ingredients:

- 4 large potatoes, peeled and thinly sliced
- 2 cups whole milk
- 1/2 cup heavy cream
- 1 1/2 cups grated Gruyère cheese
- 2 tablespoons butter
- 2 garlic cloves, minced
- 1/2 teaspoon fresh thyme
- Salt and pepper to taste

Instructions:

1. Preheat the oven to 375°F (190°C). Grease a 9x13-inch baking dish with butter.
2. In a saucepan, melt butter over medium heat. Add garlic and cook for 1 minute. Stir in milk and heavy cream, then bring to a simmer.
3. Layer the sliced potatoes in the prepared baking dish, overlapping them slightly. Pour the milk mixture over the potatoes and season with salt, pepper, and thyme.
4. Cover the dish with foil and bake for 45 minutes.
5. Remove the foil, sprinkle with Gruyère cheese, and bake for an additional 15-20 minutes, or until golden and bubbly.
6. Serve hot.

Coconut Milk Chicken Curry

Ingredients:

- 1 lb chicken breast, cubed
- 1 can (14 oz) coconut milk
- 1 onion, chopped
- 2 garlic cloves, minced
- 1 tablespoon curry powder
- 1/2 teaspoon ground turmeric
- 1/2 teaspoon ground cumin
- 1 tablespoon olive oil
- Salt and pepper to taste
- Fresh cilantro (for garnish)

Instructions:

1. In a large skillet, heat olive oil over medium heat. Add onion and garlic, and cook for 5 minutes until softened.
2. Add chicken cubes, curry powder, turmeric, cumin, salt, and pepper. Cook until the chicken is browned on all sides.
3. Stir in coconut milk, bring to a simmer, and cook for 20 minutes, or until the chicken is cooked through and the sauce has thickened.
4. Garnish with fresh cilantro and serve over rice.

Macadamia-Crusted Chicken with Milk Sauce

Ingredients:

- 4 boneless, skinless chicken breasts
- 1 cup macadamia nuts, chopped
- 1/2 cup whole milk
- 2 tablespoons butter
- 2 tablespoons flour
- 1/2 teaspoon Dijon mustard
- Salt and pepper to taste

Instructions:

1. Preheat the oven to 375°F (190°C). Place the chopped macadamia nuts on a plate.
2. Season chicken breasts with salt and pepper. Dip the chicken into the milk, then coat it with the chopped macadamia nuts.
3. In a skillet, melt butter over medium heat. Add the chicken and cook for 3-4 minutes on each side until golden. Transfer the chicken to a baking dish and bake for 15-20 minutes until cooked through.
4. In the same skillet, melt butter and add flour to make a roux. Gradually whisk in milk and Dijon mustard, cooking until the sauce thickens.
5. Serve the macadamia-crusted chicken with the milk sauce poured over the top.

Creamy Sun-Dried Tomato Pasta

Ingredients:

- 12 oz pasta of choice
- 1/2 cup sun-dried tomatoes, chopped
- 2 cups whole milk
- 1/2 cup Parmesan cheese
- 2 tablespoons olive oil
- 2 garlic cloves, minced
- Salt and pepper to taste
- Fresh basil (for garnish)

Instructions:

1. Cook the pasta according to package directions, then drain.
2. In a skillet, heat olive oil over medium heat. Add garlic and sun-dried tomatoes, cooking for 2 minutes.
3. Add milk and Parmesan cheese, stirring to combine. Let the sauce simmer for 5 minutes until it thickens.
4. Toss the cooked pasta in the sauce and season with salt and pepper.
5. Serve hot, garnished with fresh basil.

Milk-Cooked Risotto with Shrimp

Ingredients:

- 1 cup Arborio rice
- 1 lb shrimp, peeled and deveined
- 2 cups whole milk
- 1/2 cup white wine
- 1/2 cup Parmesan cheese
- 1 tablespoon butter
- 1/2 cup chopped onion
- 2 garlic cloves, minced
- Salt and pepper to taste

Instructions:

1. In a large skillet, melt butter over medium heat. Add onion and garlic, cooking for 5 minutes until softened.
2. Stir in Arborio rice and cook for 2 minutes, allowing it to lightly toast.
3. Pour in white wine and let it absorb into the rice.
4. Gradually add milk, one ladle at a time, stirring constantly. Let the liquid absorb before adding more.
5. Continue until the rice is tender and creamy, about 20 minutes.
6. In a separate pan, cook shrimp until pink, about 3 minutes per side.
7. Stir the Parmesan cheese and shrimp into the risotto, then season with salt and pepper. Serve hot.

Dairy-Free Milk Shepherd's Pie

Ingredients:

- 1 lb ground beef or lamb
- 4 large potatoes, peeled and cubed
- 1 cup dairy-free milk (such as almond milk or coconut milk)
- 1 onion, chopped
- 2 carrots, diced
- 1 cup peas
- 2 tablespoons olive oil
- 2 tablespoons tomato paste
- 1 tablespoon Worcestershire sauce (ensure it's dairy-free)
- Salt and pepper to taste
- Fresh parsley (for garnish)

Instructions:

1. Preheat the oven to 400°F (200°C).
2. Boil potatoes in salted water until soft, about 15 minutes. Drain and mash with dairy-free milk, salt, and pepper. Set aside.
3. In a large skillet, heat olive oil over medium heat. Add onion, carrots, and cook until softened, about 5 minutes.
4. Add ground meat and cook until browned. Stir in tomato paste, Worcestershire sauce, peas, salt, and pepper. Cook for another 5 minutes.
5. Transfer the meat mixture into a baking dish. Spread the mashed potatoes over the top.
6. Bake for 20 minutes until the top is golden and slightly crispy. Garnish with fresh parsley before serving.

Braised Short Ribs with Milk and Herbs

Ingredients:

- 4 bone-in beef short ribs
- 2 cups whole milk
- 1 cup beef broth
- 1 onion, chopped
- 2 garlic cloves, minced
- 2 sprigs rosemary
- 2 sprigs thyme
- 2 tablespoons olive oil
- Salt and pepper to taste

Instructions:

1. Preheat the oven to 325°F (165°C).
2. Heat olive oil in a large ovenproof pot over medium-high heat. Season the short ribs with salt and pepper, then brown on all sides, about 5 minutes per side. Remove and set aside.
3. In the same pot, add onion and garlic and cook until softened, about 5 minutes.
4. Return the short ribs to the pot and add milk, beef broth, rosemary, and thyme. Bring to a simmer.
5. Cover and transfer to the oven. Braise for 2-3 hours, or until the meat is tender and falls off the bone.
6. Serve with mashed potatoes or crusty bread.

Milk and Honey Glazed Chicken

Ingredients:

- 4 chicken breasts
- 1/4 cup honey
- 1/2 cup whole milk
- 2 tablespoons olive oil
- 1 tablespoon Dijon mustard
- 1 teaspoon garlic powder
- Salt and pepper to taste

Instructions:

1. Preheat the oven to 375°F (190°C).
2. Season chicken breasts with salt, pepper, and garlic powder.
3. In a small bowl, whisk together honey, milk, olive oil, and Dijon mustard.
4. Heat a skillet over medium-high heat and brown the chicken on both sides for 3-4 minutes.
5. Transfer the chicken to a baking dish and pour the milk and honey mixture over the top.
6. Bake for 20-25 minutes until the chicken is cooked through and the glaze is caramelized.
7. Serve with roasted vegetables or rice.

Creamy Leek and Potato Soup

Ingredients:

- 4 large potatoes, peeled and diced
- 2 leeks, cleaned and chopped
- 4 cups vegetable broth
- 1 cup dairy-free milk (such as oat milk)
- 2 tablespoons olive oil
- 2 garlic cloves, minced
- Salt and pepper to taste
- Fresh chives (for garnish)

Instructions:

1. In a large pot, heat olive oil over medium heat. Add garlic and leeks, and cook for 5 minutes until softened.
2. Add potatoes and vegetable broth, then bring to a boil. Reduce the heat and simmer for 20 minutes, or until potatoes are tender.
3. Use an immersion blender to puree the soup until smooth. If you prefer a chunkier texture, blend just half of the soup.
4. Stir in dairy-free milk, season with salt and pepper, and simmer for another 5 minutes.
5. Garnish with fresh chives and serve hot.

Roasted Chicken with Milk Sauce

Ingredients:

- 1 whole chicken (about 4 lbs)
- 2 cups whole milk
- 1 tablespoon olive oil
- 1 lemon, quartered
- 1 onion, quartered
- 4 garlic cloves
- 2 sprigs rosemary
- Salt and pepper to taste

Instructions:

1. Preheat the oven to 400°F (200°C).
2. Rub the chicken with olive oil, salt, and pepper. Place lemon, onion, garlic, and rosemary inside the chicken cavity.
3. Roast the chicken in the oven for 1 hour and 15 minutes, or until the internal temperature reaches 165°F (75°C).
4. While the chicken roasts, heat the milk in a saucepan over medium heat until it begins to simmer. Season with salt and pepper.
5. After removing the chicken from the oven, let it rest for 10 minutes before carving. Pour the milk sauce over the chicken and serve with roasted potatoes.

Milk-Cooked Pork Tenderloin

Ingredients:

- 1 lb pork tenderloin
- 2 cups whole milk
- 1 tablespoon olive oil
- 2 cloves garlic, minced
- 1 tablespoon fresh thyme, chopped
- 1 tablespoon Dijon mustard
- Salt and pepper to taste

Instructions:

1. Preheat the oven to 350°F (175°C).
2. Heat olive oil in a skillet over medium-high heat. Season the pork tenderloin with salt and pepper, then sear on all sides until golden brown, about 5 minutes.
3. Transfer the pork to a baking dish. In the same skillet, add garlic, thyme, mustard, and milk. Stir to combine.
4. Pour the milk mixture over the pork tenderloin and cover the baking dish with foil.
5. Bake for 45 minutes to 1 hour, or until the pork reaches an internal temperature of 145°F (63°C).
6. Let the pork rest for 5 minutes before slicing. Serve with the milk sauce.

Parmesan Chicken with Milk Cream Sauce

Ingredients:

- 4 chicken breasts
- 1/2 cup grated Parmesan cheese
- 1 cup whole milk
- 2 tablespoons olive oil
- 1/2 cup heavy cream
- 1 tablespoon flour
- 2 garlic cloves, minced
- Salt and pepper to taste

Instructions:

1. Preheat the oven to 375°F (190°C).
2. Season the chicken breasts with salt, pepper, and grated Parmesan cheese. In a skillet, heat olive oil over medium-high heat. Cook the chicken for 3-4 minutes per side until golden.
3. Remove the chicken and set aside. In the same skillet, add garlic and cook for 1 minute. Stir in flour and cook for another minute.
4. Gradually pour in milk and heavy cream, stirring constantly. Let the sauce simmer until thickened, about 5 minutes.
5. Return the chicken to the skillet and cover with the sauce. Bake for 20 minutes, or until the chicken is fully cooked.
6. Serve with pasta or steamed vegetables.

Creamy Vegetable Pasta Bake

Ingredients:

- 12 oz pasta (such as penne or rigatoni)
- 2 cups mixed vegetables (broccoli, bell peppers, spinach)
- 1 cup dairy-free milk
- 1/2 cup dairy-free cheese (optional)
- 1 tablespoon olive oil
- 2 garlic cloves, minced
- 1 teaspoon Italian seasoning
- Salt and pepper to taste

Instructions:

1. Preheat the oven to 375°F (190°C).
2. Cook the pasta according to package directions. Drain and set aside.
3. In a skillet, heat olive oil over medium heat. Add garlic and cook for 1 minute. Add vegetables and cook for 5-7 minutes until tender.
4. In a large baking dish, combine the cooked pasta, vegetables, dairy-free milk, and seasoning. If using dairy-free cheese, stir it in.
5. Bake for 20 minutes, or until the top is golden and bubbly. Serve hot.

Honey-Glazed Salmon with Milk Drizzle

Ingredients:

- 4 salmon fillets
- 1/4 cup honey
- 1/2 cup whole milk
- 1 tablespoon Dijon mustard
- 2 tablespoons olive oil
- Salt and pepper to taste

Instructions:

1. Preheat the oven to 375°F (190°C).
2. Season the salmon fillets with salt and pepper. Place them on a baking sheet lined with parchment paper.
3. In a small bowl, whisk together honey, milk, Dijon mustard, and olive oil. Pour the mixture over the salmon fillets.
4. Bake for 12-15 minutes, or until the salmon flakes easily with a fork.
5. Serve with the milk glaze drizzled over the top and a side of roasted vegetables or rice.

Milk and Dijon Chicken

Ingredients:

- 4 boneless chicken breasts
- 1/4 cup Dijon mustard
- 1/2 cup whole milk
- 2 tablespoons olive oil
- 1 tablespoon honey
- 1 teaspoon garlic powder
- Salt and pepper to taste
- Fresh parsley for garnish

Instructions:

1. Preheat the oven to 375°F (190°C).
2. In a small bowl, whisk together Dijon mustard, milk, honey, garlic powder, salt, and pepper.
3. Heat olive oil in a large skillet over medium-high heat. Season chicken breasts with salt and pepper, then sear them on both sides until golden brown, about 3-4 minutes per side.
4. Transfer the chicken to a baking dish and pour the milk and Dijon sauce over the top.
5. Bake for 20-25 minutes, or until the chicken is cooked through and the sauce is thickened.
6. Garnish with fresh parsley and serve with rice or roasted vegetables.

Spaghetti Carbonara with Milk

Ingredients:

- 12 oz spaghetti
- 4 slices pancetta or bacon, chopped
- 1 cup whole milk
- 2 eggs
- 1/2 cup grated Parmesan cheese
- 1 garlic clove, minced
- Salt and pepper to taste
- Fresh parsley for garnish

Instructions:

1. Cook the spaghetti according to package instructions. Drain and set aside, reserving 1/2 cup of pasta water.
2. In a skillet, cook pancetta or bacon over medium heat until crispy, about 5 minutes. Remove from heat and set aside.
3. In a bowl, whisk together eggs, milk, Parmesan, salt, and pepper.
4. Add the cooked spaghetti to the skillet with pancetta, and pour the milk and egg mixture over the pasta. Toss quickly to coat the pasta in the sauce.
5. Add reserved pasta water to achieve a creamy consistency. Season with additional salt and pepper to taste.
6. Garnish with fresh parsley and serve immediately.

Smoked Gouda and Milk Mac and Cheese

Ingredients:

- 8 oz elbow macaroni
- 1 1/2 cups whole milk
- 1/2 cup shredded smoked Gouda cheese
- 1/2 cup shredded cheddar cheese
- 2 tablespoons butter
- 2 tablespoons all-purpose flour
- 1 teaspoon Dijon mustard
- Salt and pepper to taste
- Fresh breadcrumbs for topping (optional)

Instructions:

1. Cook the macaroni according to package directions, then drain and set aside.
2. In a medium saucepan, melt butter over medium heat. Stir in flour and cook for 1-2 minutes to create a roux.
3. Gradually add the milk, whisking constantly until the mixture thickens, about 5 minutes.
4. Stir in Dijon mustard, salt, pepper, and shredded cheeses. Continue to cook, stirring occasionally, until the cheese is melted and smooth.
5. Combine the cooked macaroni with the cheese sauce. Mix well to coat the pasta.
6. For an extra crispy topping, sprinkle with fresh breadcrumbs and bake at 350°F (175°C) for 10 minutes until golden.
7. Serve immediately.

Chicken Marsala with Milk Cream Sauce

Ingredients:

- 4 boneless, skinless chicken breasts
- 1 cup whole milk
- 1/2 cup Marsala wine
- 1/2 cup chicken broth
- 1 cup mushrooms, sliced
- 2 tablespoons olive oil
- 2 tablespoons butter
- 2 tablespoons all-purpose flour
- 1 garlic clove, minced
- Salt and pepper to taste

Instructions:

1. Season the chicken breasts with salt and pepper. Heat olive oil in a skillet over medium heat and cook the chicken for 4-5 minutes per side until golden brown. Remove from the skillet and set aside.
2. In the same skillet, melt butter and sauté the garlic and mushrooms for 3-4 minutes until softened.
3. Stir in the flour and cook for 1 minute to form a roux. Gradually add Marsala wine, chicken broth, and milk, whisking to combine.
4. Return the chicken to the skillet and simmer for 10-15 minutes, or until the sauce thickens and the chicken is cooked through.
5. Serve the chicken with the creamy Marsala sauce over pasta or mashed potatoes.

Milk-Cooked Risotto Primavera

Ingredients:

- 1 cup Arborio rice
- 4 cups vegetable broth
- 1 cup whole milk
- 1 cup mixed vegetables (peas, bell peppers, zucchini, carrots)
- 1/2 cup grated Parmesan cheese
- 2 tablespoons butter
- 1 tablespoon olive oil
- 1 small onion, chopped
- 1 garlic clove, minced
- Salt and pepper to taste

Instructions:

1. In a medium saucepan, heat vegetable broth and milk together. Keep warm.
2. In a large pan, heat olive oil and butter over medium heat. Add the onion and garlic, cooking until softened, about 5 minutes.
3. Add the Arborio rice to the pan and stir to coat the rice with the oil and butter.
4. Begin adding the warm broth mixture, one ladleful at a time, stirring constantly and allowing the liquid to absorb before adding more.
5. When the rice is nearly tender (after about 20 minutes), stir in the mixed vegetables and continue cooking until the rice is fully cooked and creamy.
6. Stir in Parmesan cheese, salt, and pepper. Serve hot.

Garlic and Herb Milk-Cooked Lamb

Ingredients:

- 4 lamb chops
- 1 cup whole milk
- 2 garlic cloves, minced
- 1 tablespoon fresh rosemary, chopped
- 1 tablespoon fresh thyme, chopped
- 1 tablespoon olive oil
- Salt and pepper to taste

Instructions:

1. Season lamb chops with salt, pepper, and garlic.
2. Heat olive oil in a large skillet over medium-high heat. Brown the lamb chops on both sides, about 3-4 minutes per side.
3. Add the milk, rosemary, and thyme to the skillet. Reduce the heat to low and cover.
4. Simmer for 15-20 minutes, or until the lamb is tender and the milk sauce has thickened slightly.
5. Serve with mashed potatoes or roasted vegetables.

Creamy Chive Mashed Potatoes with Milk

Ingredients:

- 4 large potatoes, peeled and cubed
- 1/2 cup whole milk
- 1/4 cup butter
- 2 tablespoons fresh chives, chopped
- Salt and pepper to taste

Instructions:

1. Boil the potatoes in salted water until tender, about 15 minutes. Drain and return to the pot.
2. Add milk, butter, salt, and pepper. Mash the potatoes until smooth and creamy.
3. Stir in fresh chives. Serve as a side dish with roasted meats or vegetables.

Milk-Braised Veal with Vegetables

Ingredients:

- 4 veal shanks
- 2 cups whole milk
- 1 onion, chopped
- 2 carrots, peeled and chopped
- 2 celery stalks, chopped
- 2 garlic cloves, minced
- 1 tablespoon olive oil
- 1/2 cup white wine
- Salt and pepper to taste

Instructions:

1. Preheat the oven to 325°F (165°C).
2. Heat olive oil in a large, ovenproof pot over medium-high heat. Season veal shanks with salt and pepper, then brown on all sides, about 5 minutes per side.
3. Remove the veal and set aside. Add onion, carrots, celery, and garlic to the pot. Sauté for 5 minutes until softened.
4. Add white wine to deglaze the pot, scraping up any browned bits from the bottom.
5. Return the veal to the pot and add milk. Cover and transfer to the oven. Braise for 2-3 hours, or until the veal is tender.
6. Serve with mashed potatoes or a green vegetable.

Grilled Chicken with Creamy Milk Sauce

Ingredients:

- 4 boneless chicken breasts
- 1 cup whole milk
- 1/4 cup heavy cream
- 2 tablespoons butter
- 2 garlic cloves, minced
- 1 tablespoon lemon juice
- Salt and pepper to taste

Instructions:

1. Preheat the grill to medium-high heat. Season chicken breasts with salt and pepper.
2. Grill the chicken for 5-6 minutes per side, or until the internal temperature reaches 165°F (74°C).
3. While the chicken grills, melt butter in a saucepan over medium heat. Add garlic and cook for 1 minute.
4. Add milk, heavy cream, and lemon juice. Simmer until the sauce thickens, about 5 minutes.
5. Drizzle the creamy milk sauce over the grilled chicken and serve with a side of vegetables or rice.

Milk-Poached Lobster Tails

Ingredients:

- 4 lobster tails
- 2 cups whole milk
- 1/2 cup white wine
- 2 tablespoons butter
- 1 garlic clove, minced
- 1 tablespoon fresh thyme
- 1 tablespoon lemon juice
- Salt and pepper to taste
- Fresh parsley for garnish

Instructions:

1. In a large saucepan, combine whole milk, white wine, garlic, thyme, and butter. Bring to a simmer over medium heat.
2. Season the lobster tails with salt and pepper, then add them to the milk mixture. Poach the lobster tails for 6-8 minutes, or until the meat is opaque and tender.
3. Remove the lobster tails from the milk, then discard the thyme stems. Add lemon juice to the milk mixture and simmer for another 2-3 minutes to slightly reduce.
4. Serve the lobster tails drizzled with the creamy milk sauce and garnish with fresh parsley. Pair with steamed vegetables or rice.

Creamy Risotto with Peas and Milk

Ingredients:

- 1 cup Arborio rice
- 4 cups vegetable broth
- 1 cup whole milk
- 1/2 cup frozen peas
- 1/2 cup grated Parmesan cheese
- 2 tablespoons butter
- 1/2 small onion, chopped
- 2 garlic cloves, minced
- 1/4 cup white wine
- Salt and pepper to taste

Instructions:

1. In a saucepan, heat vegetable broth and milk together. Keep warm.
2. In a separate large pan, melt butter over medium heat. Add onion and garlic, cooking until softened, about 5 minutes.
3. Stir in the Arborio rice and cook for 2-3 minutes to toast the rice.
4. Add white wine and cook until mostly absorbed. Begin adding the warm broth-milk mixture, one ladleful at a time, stirring constantly and allowing the liquid to absorb before adding more.
5. When the rice is nearly tender, stir in the peas, Parmesan cheese, salt, and pepper. Cook for an additional 3-5 minutes until the rice is creamy and fully cooked.
6. Serve immediately with extra Parmesan and fresh herbs if desired.

Braised Lamb Shanks in Milk

Ingredients:

- 4 lamb shanks
- 2 cups whole milk
- 1 cup vegetable broth
- 1 onion, chopped
- 2 carrots, peeled and chopped
- 2 celery stalks, chopped
- 2 garlic cloves, minced
- 1 tablespoon fresh rosemary, chopped
- 1 tablespoon olive oil
- Salt and pepper to taste

Instructions:

1. Preheat the oven to 325°F (165°C).
2. In a large, ovenproof pot, heat olive oil over medium-high heat. Season the lamb shanks with salt and pepper, then brown them on all sides, about 5 minutes per side.
3. Remove the lamb shanks and set aside. Add onion, carrots, celery, and garlic to the pot and sauté for 5 minutes until softened.
4. Add vegetable broth, milk, and rosemary to the pot. Return the lamb shanks to the pot and bring to a simmer.
5. Cover the pot and transfer it to the oven. Braise the lamb shanks for 2-3 hours, or until the meat is tender and falling off the bone.
6. Serve the lamb with the creamy milk sauce and a side of mashed potatoes or roasted vegetables.

Milk and Tomato Braised Chicken

Ingredients:

- 4 bone-in, skinless chicken thighs
- 2 cups whole milk
- 1 can (14 oz) diced tomatoes
- 1 onion, chopped
- 2 garlic cloves, minced
- 1 teaspoon dried basil
- 1/2 teaspoon paprika
- Salt and pepper to taste
- Olive oil for searing

Instructions:

1. Season the chicken thighs with salt, pepper, and paprika. Heat olive oil in a large skillet over medium-high heat.
2. Brown the chicken thighs on both sides, about 4-5 minutes per side, then remove them from the skillet and set aside.
3. In the same skillet, sauté onion and garlic until softened, about 3-4 minutes.
4. Add the diced tomatoes, milk, basil, salt, and pepper to the skillet. Stir to combine and bring to a simmer.
5. Return the chicken thighs to the skillet, skin side up, and cover. Braise on low heat for 30-40 minutes, or until the chicken is cooked through.
6. Serve the chicken with the creamy tomato sauce over rice or pasta.

Creamy Parmesan Garlic Chicken and Rice

Ingredients:

- 4 boneless, skinless chicken breasts
- 1 cup long-grain rice
- 2 cups whole milk
- 1/2 cup grated Parmesan cheese
- 3 garlic cloves, minced
- 1 tablespoon olive oil
- 1 tablespoon butter
- Salt and pepper to taste
- Fresh parsley for garnish

Instructions:

1. Cook the rice according to package directions, then set aside.
2. Heat olive oil and butter in a large skillet over medium heat. Season chicken breasts with salt and pepper, then cook the chicken for 4-5 minutes per side, until golden brown and cooked through. Remove the chicken and set aside.
3. In the same skillet, sauté garlic for 1 minute until fragrant. Add milk and bring to a simmer.
4. Stir in the Parmesan cheese and cook until the sauce thickens, about 5 minutes.
5. Add the cooked rice to the skillet and stir to coat in the creamy sauce. Return the chicken to the skillet, placing it on top of the rice.
6. Simmer for 5-10 minutes, allowing the flavors to meld. Garnish with fresh parsley and serve immediately.

www.ingramcontent.com/pod-product-compliance
Lightning Source LLC
LaVergne TN
LVHW061956070526
838199LV00060B/4148